donna hay

for the reindeers

for Santa

christmas

thank you

Seeing as Christmas is the season of giving, I'm going to take this opportunity to thank a few of the people who have given their time and talent to this little book, which started life as a breezy idea of mine one morning and ended up taking over all our lives for several weeks. Self indulgent? Maybe, but here goes. First my right-hand man, Con Poulos, and his fellow photographers Chris Court and Ben Dearnley, who made the food look so beautiful and gave my recipes life. Next, my designer, Ann Gordon, who took a jumble of words and pictures and turned them into something that looks as if it was planned this way all along. I couldn't have coped without the fantastic ideas and sheer hard work of my food editors, Justine Poole and Steve Pearce, recipe tester Tom Frawley, and merchandiser/stylist Lucy Weight, who gathered together all those little props that make each image so special. At the business end I have to thank my editor, Sara Mulcahy, who never once lost her Christmas spirit (that's quite an achievement in the middle of June) and my copy editor, Abi Weeks, who patiently weeded out all my 'donna-isms' and made this book a joy to read as well as look at. And of course Gary Woodside and his trusty production team who ensured everything looks as good on the page as it did when it came out of the oven. Finally (I promise) special thanks go to my partner Bill, my son Angus and the rest of my extended family who always make Christmas so … eventful. Cheers.

on the cover

Sparkly festive biscuits. Follow the recipe for vanilla snap biscuits on page 60. Cut out the biscuits in your preferred shapes, use a skewer to pierce a hole for the ribbon and sprinkle with sanding sugar before baking. Donna Hay Basics sanding sugar is available from David Jones.

Fourth Estate

An imprint of HarperCollins*Publishers*

First published in Australia, New Zealand and Canada in 2005,
by Fourth Estate, an imprint of HarperCollins*Publishers*
HarperCollins*Publishers* Pty Limited
25 Ryde Road, Pymble, Sydney, NSW 2073, Australia
ABN 36 009 913 517

HarperCollins*Publishers*
31 View Road, Glenfield, Auckland 10, New Zealand
2 Bloor Street East, 20th Floor, Toronto, Ontario M4W 1A8, Canada

DONNA HAY CHRISTMAS Copyright © Donna Hay 2005
Design copyright © Donna Hay 2005
Photographs copyright © Con Poulos 2005 pages 1,4,7, 9, 11, 12, 13, 15, 16, 17, 19, 21, 22, 23, 25, 30-33, 34-41, 43, 44, 45-53, 55-63, 80
© Chris Court pages 11, 12, 29, 30, 44
© Ben Dearnley pages 21, 27
Art Direction: Ann Gordon for *designmecca*
Editor: Sara Mulcahy
Copy Editor: Abi Weeks
Food Editors: Justine Poole, Steve Pearce, Tom Frawley
Merchandising: Lucy Weight

Reproduction by News Magazines Prepress, Sydney, Australia.
Produced in Hong Kong by Phoenix Offset on 157gsm Chinese Matt Art.
Printed in China.

National Library of Australia Cataloguing-in-Publication data:
Hay, Donna.
Donna Hay Christmas.
Includes index.
ISBN 0 7322 8333 7.
1. Christmas cookery. I. Poulos, Con. II. Title.
641.5686

Library and Archives Canada Cataloguing in Publication:
Hay, Donna
Donna Hay Christmas / Donna Hay. – 1st Canadian ed.
ISBN-13: 978-0-00-200753-5
ISBN-10: 0-00-200753-3
1. Christmas cookery. I. Title.
TX739.2.C45H39 2005   641.5'686   C2005-904448-9

HarperCollins books may be purchased for educational, business or sales promotional use. For information in Australia, New Zealand or Canada, please write to the Special Markets Department of HarperCollins in that country.

05 06 07 08 09 / 10 9 8 7 6 5 4 3 2 1

donna hay

christmas

simple recipes ✳ menu planners

photography by con poulos

FOURTH ESTATE

contents

introduction

We all look forward to this special time of year. It's about family, friends, gifts, parties … and food, which is where that vaguely uneasy feeling can start to set in. So that's why I've compiled this book. There's a traditional menu with turkey and trimmings, a modern menu full of new ideas, and a collection of simple recipes for the truly time-poor. I've also included menu planners for each chapter to ensure you'll be spending the minimum amount of time in the kitchen. So whatever kind of festive season you're anticipating, there's something here to suit. Welcome to your most fuss-free Christmas ever.

Donna

traditional christmas

If you're hosting the family Christmas, take inspiration
from your grandmother's kitchen for these festive classics.
And remember, many hands make light work.

NIBBLES

chilli spiced nuts ✳ saffron risotto cakes
✳ chive frittatas with smoked salmon
✳ thyme and brandy pâté

MAINS

perfect roasted turkey ✳ roast pork loin
✳ glazed ham

SIDES

honey and spice glazed vegetables
garlic roast asparagus ✳ red onion and potato gratin
✳ peas with pancetta and mint

DESSERTS

christmas pudding ✳ grandma's fruit cake
✳ brandy and vanilla custard

combined menu serves 12–16

saffron risotto cakes

1 pinch saffron threads
2 tablespoons boiling water
1 quantity basic risotto (see glossary), chilled
50g (1¾ oz) mozzarella, cut into 16 pieces
vegetable oil for shallow-frying

Place the saffron threads in a heatproof bowl, pour over the boiling water and set aside for 10 minutes. Add the saffron threads and liquid to the risotto and mix to combine. Take a heaped tablespoonful of risotto and mould it in the palm of your hand. Place a piece of mozzarella in the middle and press the risotto over to enclose, shaping it into a cake. Repeat with the remaining mixture. Refrigerate the risotto cakes until needed. Heat the oil in a saucepan over medium heat. When oil is hot, shallow-fry the cakes for 2–3 minutes or until golden. Drain on absorbent paper. Makes 16.

chive frittatas with smoked salmon

6 eggs
1 cup (8 fl oz) (single or pouring) cream
¾ cup grated cheddar cheese
2 tablespoons chopped chives
sea salt and cracked black pepper
topping
½ cup sour cream
80g (2¾ oz) cream cheese, softened
1½ tablespoons lemon juice
50g (1¾ oz) sliced smoked salmon
snipped chives, extra, to garnish

Preheat oven to 160°C (320°F). Place the eggs, cream, cheddar, chives, salt and pepper in a bowl and mix to combine. Pour into 12 x ½ cup (4 fl oz) capacity greased muffin tins and bake for 15 minutes or until set. Remove from the tins and cool slightly. To serve, combine the sour cream, cream cheese and lemon juice in a bowl and place a teaspoonful on top of each frittata. Top with a small piece of smoked salmon and garnish with the extra chives. Makes 12.

thyme and brandy pâté

20g (¾ oz) butter
2 teaspoons olive oil
2 small brown onions, chopped
2 cloves garlic, crushed
4 teaspoons thyme leaves
600g (1⅓ lb) chicken livers, trimmed
4 tablespoons brandy
100g (3½ oz) butter, extra, softened
⅔ cup (5 fl oz) (single or pouring) cream
sea salt and cracked black pepper
1 cup (8 fl oz) canned chicken consommé
2 teaspoons gelatine powder
¼ cup juniper berries

Heat a large non-stick frying pan over medium heat. Add the butter, oil, onions, garlic and thyme and cook for 1 minute or until soft. Add the livers and cook for a further minute. Pour in the brandy and cook until evaporated. Process the liver mixture with the extra butter and the cream until smooth. Season well with salt and pepper. Push the mixture through a sieve and spoon into eight ½ cup (4 fl oz) capacity dishes. In a small pan, warm the consommé over low heat. Add the gelatine and stir until dissolved. Allow to cool slightly. Place a few juniper berries on each pâté and pour in the consommé to fill the dishes. Refrigerate until firm. Makes 8.

chilli spiced nuts

2 tablespoons vegetable or peanut oil
2 teaspoons mild ground chilli
4 teaspoons smoky sweet paprika
2 teaspoons sea salt
2 teaspoons ground cumin
3 cups mixed nuts of your choice

Heat a frying pan over medium–high heat. Add the oil, chilli, paprika, salt and cumin and stir for 2 minutes or until the spices are fragrant. Add the nuts and stir for 5 minutes or until the nuts are golden. Makes 3 cups.

saffron risotto cakes

thyme and brandy pâté

chive frittatas with smoked salmon

chilli spiced nuts

11

perfect roasted turkey

roast pork loin

glazed ham

13

perfect roasted turkey

3kg (6½ lb) turkey
60g (2 oz) butter
2 quantities stuffing (for stuffing recipes, see page 16)
vegetable oil, for brushing
1½ cups (12 fl oz) chicken stock

Preheat the oven to 180°C (355°F). Wash the turkey, pat dry and tuck the wings underneath. Gently push a spoon between the skin of the turkey and the breast meat to release the skin from the flesh (take care not to split the skin). Using your fingers, evenly distribute the butter under the skin. Loosely fill the turkey cavity with stuffing. Close the cavity with a thin metal skewer and secure the legs with kitchen string. Lightly brush the turkey with oil and place on a greased rack in a baking dish filled with the stock. Cover with greased aluminium foil and roast for 1 hour 30 minutes. Remove the foil and cook for a further 30 minutes or until the skin is golden and the turkey is cooked when tested with a skewer. Rest the turkey for 20 minutes before carving. Serves 6.

roast pork loin

2kg (4½ lb) loin of pork
2 quantities stuffing (for stuffing recipes, see page 16)
vegetable oil, for rubbing
sea salt
10 small apples

Preheat the oven to 220°C (425°F). With the point of a sharp knife, score the skin of the pork at 1.5cm (⅔ in) intervals. Lay the loin out flat, place the stuffing down the middle and roll up. Secure with kitchen string and rub the skin with oil and salt. Place the meat on a rack in a baking dish. Bake for 30 minutes. Reduce the heat to 200°C (390°F) and bake for a further 30 minutes. Make a cut around the circumference of the apples, place with the pork on the baking rack and cook for a further 20 minutes or until the pork is cooked to your liking. Slice and serve with the apples. Serves 6–8.

glazed ham

8kg (18 lb) leg ham
cloves for studding
glaze
½ cup (4 fl oz) fresh orange juice
⅓ cup brown sugar
¼ cup dijon mustard
⅓ cup (2½ fl oz) honey

Preheat the oven to 190°C (375°F). Remove the skin from the ham and discard. Score the fat in a diamond pattern (see glossary). Stud a clove in the middle of each diamond. Place the ham in a baking dish lined with a few layers of non-stick baking (parchment) paper.

To make the glaze, place the orange juice, sugar, mustard and honey in a small saucepan over medium heat. Simmer, stirring occasionally, for 15 minutes or until thickened. Brush the ham with the glaze and bake for 10 minutes. Glaze again and bake for another 10 minutes. Repeat and bake for a final 10 minutes or until golden. Allow the ham to stand for 5 minutes before carving. Serves 10–12.

perfectly cooked pork

+ **timing is everything** It isn't necessary to cook pork until it is completely dried out, as was the fashion in the past. (According to an old wives' tale, overcooking pork guarded against disease.) Try cooking your pork to medium rather than well done and taste the difference.
+ **complementary flavours** Pork goes well with many flavours; apple and herbs (such as sage, parsley, thyme and rosemary) can be placed under the pork before baking or incorporated into the stuffing.
+ For more tips on cooking pork, see page 52.

couscous stuffing

Combine 1 cup couscous with 1¼ cups (10 fl oz) boiling chicken or vegetable stock. Cover and stand until the stock is absorbed. Add ¼ cup chopped fresh herbs (such as parsley, basil, chives, thyme or rosemary), 2 chopped cooked onions or leeks and cracked black pepper and sea salt and mix well. Use for meat or fish.

lemon and herb stuffing

Mix 3 cups fresh breadcrumbs with 2 teaspoons finely grated lemon rind, ¼ cup chopped mixed fresh herbs (such as parsley, basil, thyme, rosemary or chives), 60g (2 oz) soft butter, sea salt and cracked black pepper. Use for chicken, veal or lamb; double the quantities for a turkey.

caramelised onion stuffing

Cook 1 tablespoon olive oil, 1 tablespoon butter and 4 sliced red onions in a small pan over low heat for 10 minutes or until the onions are soft and golden. Add 3–4 cups fresh breadcrumbs and 1 tablespoon chopped herbs (sage, thyme, oregano or rosemary) and mix well. Use for beef, veal, lamb or chicken.

easy herb stuffing

Cook 2 teaspoons olive oil and 1 finely chopped onion in a frying pan over medium–high heat for 5 minutes. Add 3 cups fresh white breadcrumbs, 1½ teaspoons dried mixed herbs, 30g (1 oz) soft butter, sea salt and cracked black pepper and mix well. Use for chicken or lamb; double the quantities for a turkey.

white wine and thyme mustard

2 tablespoons black or brown mustard seeds
6 tablespoons yellow mustard seeds
$\frac{1}{3}$ cup (2½ fl oz) white wine vinegar
$\frac{1}{3}$ cup (2½ fl oz) chardonnay
¼ cup (2 fl oz) honey
1 tablespoon lemon juice
1 teaspoon lemon thyme leaves
sea salt and cracked black pepper

Place the mustard seeds in a non-metallic bowl and pour over the vinegar and wine. Cover and stand overnight. Place the mustard seed mixture in a small food processor or mortar and pestle with the honey, lemon juice, thyme, salt and pepper. Grind the mixture until almost smooth. Spoon into a hot sterilised jar and seal. Allow to cool and store in the refrigerator for up to 1 week. Makes approximately 1 cup.

cheat's cranberry sauce

500g (1 lb) frozen cranberries
2 cups caster (superfine) sugar
¼ cup (2 fl oz) malt vinegar
¼ cup (2 fl oz) port

Preheat the oven to 200°C (390°F). Place the cranberries in a baking dish, add the sugar, vinegar and port and toss well to combine. Cook for 30 minutes or until the cranberries are soft and the sauce is thickened. Spoon into hot sterilised jars and store in the fridge for up to 2 weeks. Serve warm or cold with roast turkey or pork. Makes 3 cups (24 fl oz).

beetroot and balsamic relish

750g (1½ lb) beetroot, peeled and coarsely grated
1 brown onion, finely chopped
2 cups (16 fl oz) balsamic vinegar
1 cup (8 fl oz) water
3 teaspoons yellow mustard seeds
2½ cups granulated sugar
2 cloves
5cm (2 in) piece orange rind
sea salt and cracked black pepper

Place the beetroot, onion, vinegar, water, mustard seeds, sugar, cloves, orange rind, salt and pepper in a large deep frying pan or jam pan. Place over medium heat, cover and bring to the boil. Cook for 30 minutes or until the beetroot is soft and the liquid has reduced and thickened slightly. Spoon into hot sterilised jars and seal. Allow to cool and store in the fridge for up to 2 months. Makes 5 cups (2 pints).

basic gravy

pan juices from roast chicken, turkey, lamb, beef or pork
10–12 ice cubes
2½ tablespoons plain (all-purpose) flour
stock, wine or water, to add to pan juices

Remove the roasted meat or poultry from the baking dish and keep warm. Pour the pan juices into a jug with the ice cubes and allow the fat to solidify. Skim off 2 tablespoons of the solidified fat and return to the baking dish. Discard the remaining fat, reserving the pan juices. Add the flour to the fat in the baking dish and stir over medium heat for 4–5 minutes or until the paste is a light golden colour. Make the pan juices in the jug up to 2 cups (16 fl oz) with the stock, wine or water. Slowly whisk the liquid into the flour mixture until a smooth consistency. Stir over medium heat until the gravy comes to the boil and thickens. Makes 2 cups (16 fl oz).

white wine and thyme mustard

beetroot and balsamic relish

cheat's cranberry sauce

basic gravy

garlic roast asparagus

2–3 bunches asparagus, trimmed
olive oil
4 cloves garlic, sliced
shredded rind of 1 lemon
lemon juice, to serve
shaved parmesan cheese, to serve

Preheat the oven to 180ºC (355ºF). Place the asparagus in a baking dish. Sprinkle over a generous amount of olive oil and toss with the garlic and lemon rind. Cover and bake for 25–35 minutes or until the asparagus is tender. Serve with a squeeze of lemon and the shaved parmesan. Serves 8.

honey and spice glazed vegetables

1kg (2¼ lb) butternut pumpkin, cut into wedges
1kg (2¼ lb) sweet potato, peeled and quartered
4 parsnips, peeled and halved
2 celeriac (celery root), peeled and quartered
2–3 tablespoons vegetable oil
honey and spice glaze
½ cup (4 fl oz) honey, warmed
1 teaspoon ground chilli
1 teaspoon ground sweet paprika
1 teaspoon ground cumin
1 teaspoon ground coriander (cilantro)
sea salt and cracked black pepper

Preheat oven to 180°C (355ºF). Place the vegetables into 2 baking dishes lined with non-stick baking (parchment) paper. Toss the vegetables with the oil and bake for 45 minutes or until just tender. To make the honey and spice glaze, mix together the honey, chilli, paprika, cumin, coriander, salt and pepper. Brush generously over the vegetables and bake for a further 10 minutes or until the vegetables are golden. Serves 8.

red onion and potato gratin

8 desiree potatoes, thinly sliced
4 red onions, thinly sliced
1 tablespoon thyme leaves
1 cup finely grated parmesan cheese
sea salt and cracked black pepper
1 cup (8 fl oz) (single or pouring) cream
½ cup (4 fl oz) beef stock

Preheat the oven to 200ºC (390ºF). Place a layer of potato in the bases of two 1 litre (32 fl oz) capacity ovenproof dishes. Top with a third of the onion, thyme, parmesan, salt and pepper. Repeat with the remaining ingredients, finishing with a layer of potato. Top with any remaining parmesan and thyme. Combine the cream and stock in a bowl and pour over the layered potato. Cover the dishes with foil, place on a baking tray and bake for 20 minutes. Remove the foil and cook for a further 30 minutes or until the potato is tender and the top is golden. Serves 8.

peas with pancetta and mint

½ cup (4 fl oz) chicken stock
5 cups fresh or frozen peas (2kg/4½ lb in the pod)
12 slices pancetta (see glossary), chopped
60g (2 oz) butter
¼ cup shredded mint leaves
cracked black pepper

Bring the stock to the boil in a saucepan over medium to high heat. Add the peas, cover and cook for 5 minutes or until tender. Meanwhile, place the pancetta in a frying pan over high heat and stir for 2 minutes or until crisp. Toss the pancetta, butter, mint and pepper with the peas and serve immediately. Serves 8.

garlic roast asparagus

red onion and potato gratin

honey and spice glazed vegetables

peas with pancetta and mint

21

christmas pudding

brandy and vanilla custard

grandma's fruit cake

christmas pudding

¾ cup sultanas

1 cup currants

1½ cups raisins, halved

¾ cup chopped pitted prunes or dates

⅔ cup candied mixed peel

⅔ cup slivered almonds

½ cup (4 fl oz) brandy or sherry

250g (8¾ oz) butter, softened

¼ cup brown sugar

¼ cup granulated sugar

3 eggs

1 cup plain (all-purpose) flour, sifted

1 teaspoon ground cinnamon

1 teaspoon mixed spice

250g (8¾ oz) fresh breadcrumbs

⅔ cup (5 fl oz) milk

1 x 80cm (30 in) square of calico cloth (see glossary)

plain (all-purpose) flour, extra

Place the sultanas, currants, raisins, prunes, mixed peel, almonds and brandy in a bowl and allow to soak for at least 4 hours. Place the butter, brown sugar and sugar in the bowl of an electric mixer and beat until light and creamy. Gradually add the eggs and beat well. Transfer the butter mixture to a large bowl. Add the fruit mixture, flour, cinnamon, mixed spice, breadcrumbs and milk and mix with a wooden spoon until well combined. Wearing rubber gloves, dip the calico in boiling water and carefully squeeze to remove any excess water. While the cloth is still hot, rub in the extra flour to form a skin around the pudding. Place the fruit mixture in the middle and gather up the ends of the cloth firmly around it. Tie the cloth with kitchen string as close to the mixture as possible, making a loop at the end of the string. Place the pudding in a saucepan of boiling water and boil for 4 hours 30 minutes, adding more water if necessary. Remove the pudding from the pan and hang on a broomstick over a sink. Allow to cool. Store in the fridge for up to 2 months. To reheat, boil for 45 minutes and drain for 5 minutes. Unwrap and serve with brandy and vanilla custard (right) or brandy butter (see page 64). Serves 12.

brandy and vanilla custard

2 tablespoons cornflour (cornstarch)

3 cups (24 fl oz) (single or pouring) cream

¼ cup (2 fl oz) brandy

1 split, scraped vanilla bean (see glossary)

6 egg yolks

⅓ cup caster (superfine) sugar

Mix the cornflour with a little cream until smooth. Set aside. Heat the cream, brandy and vanilla in a pan over medium heat until warm. Whisk together the yolks and sugar. Slowly whisk the egg and the cornflour mixtures into the cream. Stir over low heat for 4 minutes or until thick. Makes 3½ cups (28 fl oz).

grandma's fruit cake

3 cups raisins

1½ cups sultanas

1 cup currants

¾ cup chopped dates

1 cup slivered almonds

¾ cup (6 fl oz) brandy

250g (8¾ oz) butter, softened

1¼ cups brown sugar

4 eggs

2¼ cups plain (all-purpose) flour, sifted

¼ teaspoon bicarbonate of soda (baking soda)

1 teaspoon ground cinnamon

2–3 tablespoons brandy, extra

Place the fruit and nuts in a bowl and pour over the brandy. Cover and allow to soak overnight. Preheat the oven to 140°C (285°F). Place the butter and sugar in the bowl of an electric mixer and beat until light and creamy. Gradually add the eggs and beat well. Place the butter and fruit mixtures, flour, bicarbonate of soda and cinnamon in a bowl and stir to combine. Line a 20cm (8 in) square cake tin with two layers of non-stick baking (parchment) paper. Spoon in the mixture and bake for 2 hours or until cooked. Pour over the extra brandy while the cake is hot. Cool in the tin. Serves 12.

traditional menu: planning ahead

+ **turkey cooking guide**
*20 minutes at 180°C
(355ºF) per 500g (1 lb)*
To ensure a perfectly
roasted turkey, cook
it covered for most of
the oven time to keep
the outer parts from
becoming dry. Remove
the cover in the last
30 minutes to brown
and crisp up the skin.
Alternatively, place some
softened butter between
the skin and the breast
to keep the meat moist.

up to 2 months before

☐ Make the Christmas pudding, wrap tightly in plastic wrap and store in the refrigerator.

☐ Make the grandma's fruit cake, store in an airtight container or wrapped in plastic wrap in a cake tin. Keep in a cool place.

3–4 weeks before

☐ Order the turkey, pork and ham and arrange a time and date for collection.

☐ Make the white wine and thyme mustard and store in an airtight container in the refrigerator.

2 weeks before

☐ Make the cheat's cranberry sauce and store in the refrigerator.

☐ Make the ham glaze and store in the refrigerator.

☐ Make the beetroot and balsamic relish and store in the refrigerator.

1 week before

☐ Decide on and purchase the wines, aperitifs, beers and soft drinks to go with your menu.

3 days before

☐ Purchase all remaining fresh fruit and vegetables required for your menu.

☐ Choose your stuffings for the turkey and pork, prepare and refrigerate until required. Don't stuff the pork or turkey until the day you are cooking it.

2 days before

☐ Make the saffron risotto cakes and refrigerate until ready to cook. You can also cook these ahead of time and reheat, covered, in a warm oven or microwave.

☐ Make the thyme and brandy pâté, cover and refrigerate. Stand at room temperature for 10 minutes before serving.

1 day before

☐ Make the red onion and potato gratin and refrigerate until required. Reheat covered with aluminium foil.

☐ Cook the chilli spiced nuts. Store in an airtight container. Before serving, warm in the microwave for 20–30 seconds.

☐ Glaze and cook the ham as you probably won't have room in the oven on the day. Reheat the ham on the day in a 190°C (375°F) oven for 20 minutes.

on the day

- ☐ Prepare the turkey and pork, fill with the stuffings and place on baking dishes ready to roast.

- ☐ Cook the chive frittatas and store at room temperature. Add the cream cheese and smoked salmon just before serving.

- ☐ Cook the garlic roast asparagus and store in the refrigerator. Reheat, covered, in a hot oven or microwave or serve at room temperature.

- ☐ Place the turkey in the oven 2½ hours before serving.

- ☐ Place the pork in the oven 1½ hours before serving.

- ☐ Place the honey and spice glazed vegetables in the oven 45 minutes before serving. If you are short of oven space, use the smallest oven trays you have and place things side by side. Alternatively, cook the vegetables in a covered barbecue outside.

- ☐ Cook the peas with pancetta and mint and keep covered with the saucepan lid to keep the peas warm.

- ☐ Before sitting down to eat, place the Christmas pudding in a large saucepan of boiling water for 45 minutes to reheat.

tips + tricks

+ **will the turkey fit in the oven?** If you're not sure, measure the space from the bottom shelf to the top of the oven and the baking dish before you go shopping. Take these measurements and a tape measure to the butcher's or supermarket; you might look strange measuring up a turkey, but it'll save worse embarrassment on Christmas day. An alternative is to cook the turkey in a covered barbecue, or buy boneless turkey breasts that will fit on a baking tray.

+ **not enough space in your oven?** You can cook the turkey the day before and serve it cold. Cook the pork and vegetables on the day and serve them hot. Don't reheat cooked turkey or pork, as it will dry out. And don't partially cook meat or poultry or you risk bacterial contamination. Vegetables that take an hour or so can be roasted ahead of time and reheated later.

modern christmas

Create a few new traditions with a simple yet stylish menu
that will give your festive season a contemporary twist.

NIBBLES
oysters with lemon and crispy capers

✳· goat's cheese and dill quiches

✳· chicken and rocket sandwiches

STARTER
✳· wok-fried salt and pepper crab

MAIN
✳· roast beef with horseradish sauce

SIDES
tomato, basil and olive salad ✳· roast kipfler

potato salad ✳· prawn and cucumber salad

DESSERTS
frozen white christmas

✳· honey and nutmeg biscuits

combined menu serves 8

oysters with lemon and crispy capers

goat's cheese and dill quiches

chicken and rocket sandwiches

oysters with lemon and crispy capers

1 tablespoon olive oil
50g (1¾ oz) butter
¼ cup salted capers, rinsed and drained (see glossary)
1 clove garlic, crushed
1 tablespoon lemon rind
2 green onions (scallions), thinly sliced
2 dozen oysters

Heat a small frying pan over high heat. Add the oil and butter and cook for 1 minute or until the butter is melted. Add the capers and garlic and cook for 2–3 minutes or until the capers are crispy. Add the lemon rind and green onions and spoon over the oysters to serve. Serves 8.

+ **cook's note** Use only the freshest Pacific or rock oysters available on the day of purchase.

goat's cheese and dill quiches

3 sheets shortcrust pastry or 600g (1⅓ lb) ready-made
   shortcrust pastry (see glossary)
filling
80g (2¾ oz) goat's cheese
¼ cup dill sprigs
4 egg yolks
1⅓ cups (10½ fl oz) (single or pouring) cream
½ teaspoon finely grated lemon rind
sea salt and cracked black pepper

Preheat the oven to 160°C (320°F). Cut each pastry sheet into 4 squares. On a baking tray lined with baking (parchment) paper, line 12 greased egg rings with the pastry and trim any excess. Place the goat's cheese and dill in the cases. Whisk the egg yolks, cream, lemon rind, salt and pepper. Pour the egg mixture into the cases. Bake for 30 minutes or until the top is golden and the filling is set. Remove the egg rings to serve. Makes 12.

chicken and rocket sandwiches

3 chicken breast fillets, cooked and chopped
1 cup whole egg mayonnaise
⅓ cup sour cream
2 cups shredded rocket (arugula) leaves
sea salt and cracked black pepper
12 slices white bread, crusts removed

Place the chicken, mayonnaise, sour cream, rocket, salt and pepper in a bowl and mix to combine. Spread the chicken mixture over half the bread slices and top with remaining bread slices. Cut the sandwiches into 3 pieces. Cover with plastic wrap until serving. Serves 8.

wok-fried salt and pepper crab

3 x 800g–1kg (1¾–2¼ lb) large raw mud crabs, cleaned
4 tablespoons peanut oil
1 tablespoon sesame oil
1 tablespoon flaked sea salt
3 teaspoons cracked black pepper
3 small red chillies, seeded and finely chopped
lemon wedges to serve

Cut each crab into eight pieces. Crack the large claws with the back of a knife or a crab cracker. Place a large wok or deep frying pan over high heat. Add the oils and crab claws and cook for 6–8 minutes. Add the remaining crab, salt, pepper and chillies and cook for 2 minutes or until fragrant. Cover and cook for 6–8 minutes or until the shells are bright orange. Serve the crab immediately with lemon wedges, crab crackers, crab picks, forks and finger bowls. Serves 8.

+ **cook's note** In place of the mud crabs, you can use whole small langoustine, blue swimmer crabs, yabby tails, marron tails or whole unpeeled prawns (shrimp) with the heads removed. Adjust the cooking times to suit.

wok-fried salt and pepper crab

roast beef with horseradish sauce

tomato, basil and olive salad   roast kipfler potato salad

roast beef with horseradish sauce

1.2kg (2½ lb) long beef fillet, tied with kitchen string
olive oil, for brushing
3 teaspoons sea salt
2 teaspoons cracked black pepper
3 tablespoons chopped thyme leaves
1½ tablespoons finely grated lemon rind
4 cloves garlic, crushed
3 tablespoons olive oil
½ cup (4 fl oz) water
½ cup (4 fl oz) white wine
½ cup (4 fl oz) beef stock
3 teaspoons horseradish cream

Preheat the oven to 200ºC (390ºF). Brush the beef with oil. Heat a baking tray over medium heat on the stove and brown the fillet for 3 minutes each side. Combine the salt, pepper, thyme, lemon, garlic and oil and brush over the beef. Roast in the oven for 30 minutes for medium–rare or until cooked to your liking. Set aside. Place the baking tray over medium heat, add the water, wine, stock and horseradish and stir to combine. Bring to a simmer and cook for 2–3 minutes or until thickened. Serve the sauce with the beef. Serves 8.

tomato, basil and olive salad

4 thick slices bread, torn into small pieces
1½ tablespoons olive oil
80g (2¾ oz) rocket (arugula) leaves
5 tomatoes, thickly sliced
5 bocconcini (see glossary), torn
2 tablespoons finely chopped black olives or tapenade
2 tablespoons basil leaves
2 tablespoons olive oil, extra
2 tablespoons red wine vinegar

Preheat the oven to 200ºC (390ºF). Toss the bread with the oil, place on a baking tray and cook for 10 minutes. Top the rocket with tomatoes, bocconcini, olives, basil and croutons. Combine oil and vinegar and spoon over to serve. Serves 8.

roast kipfler potato salad

1kg (2¼ lb) kipfler potatoes (see glossary), halved
1 tablespoon olive oil
sea salt and cracked black pepper
100g (3½ oz) baby spinach leaves
parmesan dressing
¼ cup whole egg mayonnaise
¼ cup finely grated parmesan
2 tablespoons white wine vinegar
½ cup chopped mint leaves
½ cup chopped flat-leaf parsley leaves
¼ cup chopped green onions (scallions)

Preheat the oven to 200ºC (390ºF). To make the parmesan dressing, combine the mayonnaise, parmesan, vinegar, mint, parsley and green onions. Set aside.

Place the potatoes in a baking dish with the oil, sea salt and cracked black pepper and toss to combine. Roast the potatoes for 40 minutes or until golden. To serve, toss with the baby spinach and the parmesan dressing. Serves 8.

prawn and cucumber salad

375g (13 oz) rice (stick) noodles (see glossary)
2 large cucumbers, shredded
½ cup mint leaves, roughly chopped
½ cup basil leaves, roughly chopped
½ cup coriander (cilantro) leaves
1 long red chilli, deseeded and chopped
½ cup (4 fl oz) lemon juice
2 tablespoons caster (superfine) sugar
3 tablespoons fish sauce
1.5kg (3½ lb) cooked peeled prawns (shrimp), tails intact

Place the noodles in a large bowl and cover with boiling water. Allow to stand for 6–8 minutes or until soft, then drain. Combine the noodles, cucumber, mint, basil, coriander, chilli, lemon juice, sugar, fish sauce and prawns and toss to combine. Serves 8.

prawn and cucumber salad

frozen white christmas

200g (7 oz) dried sweetened cranberries (see glossary)
¼ cup (2 fl oz) brandy
4 cups (1 litre/32 fl oz) thickened cream
2 cups icing (confectioner's) sugar, sifted
2 teaspoons vanilla extract
2 tablespoons brandy, extra
200g (7 oz) white chocolate, melted
fresh blackberries and raspberries, to serve
icing (confectioner's) sugar, extra, for dusting

Place the cranberries and brandy in a bowl and soak for
4 hours or overnight. Place the cream and icing sugar in
a bowl and whip until soft peaks form. Fold through the
cranberry mixture, vanilla and extra brandy. Spoon into
8 x 1 cup (8 fl oz) capacity greased moulds and freeze for
6 hours or until firm. Remove from the moulds and place
on a baking tray lined with non-stick baking (parchment)
paper. Drizzle with the melted chocolate and return to the
freezer. Serve with berries dusted with icing sugar. Serves 8.

+ **cook's note** Find dried sweetened cranberries in the dried
   fruit section of large supermarkets and health food stores.

honey and nutmeg biscuits

175g (6 oz) cold butter, cubed
¾ cup caster (superfine) sugar
½ teaspoon vanilla extract
2 cups plain (all-purpose) flour
¼ cup (2 fl oz) honey
1 egg
icing
1½ cups icing (confectioners) sugar, sifted
2 teaspoons honey
1–1½ tablespoons water
freshly grated nutmeg

Place the butter, sugar and vanilla in the bowl of a food
processor and process until smooth. Add the flour, honey
and egg and process again to form a smooth dough. Knead
the dough lightly, enclose in plastic wrap and refrigerate
for 30 minutes. Preheat oven to 180°C (355°F). Roll
tablespoons of the mixture into 4cm (1½ in) rounds and
flatten slightly. Place the biscuits on baking trays lined with
non-stick baking (parchment) paper. Bake the biscuits for
12–15 minutes or until dark golden. Cool on wire racks.

   To make the icing, combine the icing sugar, honey and
enough water until smooth and thick. Top the biscuits with
the icing and sprinkle with the nutmeg. Store in an airtight
container for up to 2 days. Makes 26.

frozen white christmas   honey and nutmeg biscuits

modern menu: planning ahead

2 weeks before

- ☐ Order the crabs, prawns, oysters and beef. The beef can be collected up to 3 days prior to cooking and the seafood should be collected 1–2 days before or as close to serving as possible.

1 week before

- ☐ Make the honey and nutmeg biscuits (don't ice them) and place in an airtight container.

- ☐ If you are using homemade pastry for the goat's cheese and dill quiches, make the pastry, wrap in a few layers of plastic wrap and refrigerate until ready to use.

- ☐ Decide on and purchase the wines, aperitifs, beers and soft drinks to go with your menu.

2 days before

- ☐ Ice the honey and nutmeg biscuits and return to the airtight container.

- ☐ Make the goat's cheese and dill quiches and store in an airtight container in the refrigerator. To reheat on the day, place on baking trays and cook at 180°C (355°F) for 8 minutes or until warm.

- ☐ Make the frozen white christmas. Cover the ice cream with plastic wrap so it doesn't take on any other food aromas from the freezer.

- ☐ Make the croutons for the tomato, basil and olive salad and store in an airtight container.

1 day before

- ☐ Make the filling for the chicken and rocket sandwiches, cover and refrigerate.

- ☐ Make the parmesan dressing for the roast kipfler potato salad and refrigerate until required.

- ☐ Trim the beef and secure with string, ready to roast. Store loosely wrapped in the refrigerator. Measure out and prepare all the ingredients for the horseradish sauce and keep on a tray in the refrigerator until needed.

- ☐ Remove the frozen white christmas from the moulds. Place on a tray lined with baking (parchment) paper. Spoon over the chocolate and return to the freezer.

- ☐ Prepare, wash and chop the mud crabs into 8 pieces each for the wok-fried salt and pepper crab. Store the crabs in the refrigerator, covered with a damp clean tea towel or cloth.

+ **roasting beef**

When roasting beef it is important to brown the outside of the beef well to ensure that the meat is sealed and the juices are locked in. The browning also gives the beef extra flavour.

+ **cooking guide**

Preheat the oven to 180°C (355°F). For a thick cut of beef, cook 15 minutes for every 500g for rare; 20 minutes for medium; and 25–30 minutes for well done.

on the day

- [ ] Make the lemon and crispy caper dressing for the oysters and stand at room temperature until ready to spoon over the chilled oysters.

- [ ] Assemble the chicken and rocket sandwiches and cover with a slightly damp tea towel or plastic wrap to prevent the bread from drying out.

- [ ] Prepare and assemble the prawn and cucumber salad and refrigerate until required.

- [ ] Prepare and roast the potatoes for the roast kipfler potato salad 1 hour before serving. Cover the potatoes after cooking to keep them warm.

- [ ] Brown the beef and place in the oven 40 minutes before serving. Alternatively, you can roast the beef and make the sauce the day before. Then reheat the sauce in a small saucepan over low heat.

- [ ] Assemble the tomato, basil and olive salad and toss the croutons through just before serving to ensure they stay crisp.

- [ ] Place a batch of the honey and nutmeg biscuits on a plate and sprinkle with freshly grated nutmeg. Keep the rest in the airtight container until ready to eat.

tips + tricks

+ **crabs** Choose crabs that are heavy for their size with a fresh, sweet sea smell. Store live or uncooked crabs in the refrigerator, covered in a damp clean tea towel or cloth, for up to 2 days.

+ **prawns** Choose firm prawns that have a bright colour and no discoloration around the legs or head. Store prawns in their shells for 2–3 days in an airtight container in the refrigerator. Storing them in their shells keeps the moisture and flavour in the prawns. Avoid storing them on ice; as the ice melts, the prawns will sit in water, making the prawn flesh taste watery.

+ **oysters** Choose plump creamy oysters with a fresh, sweet sea smell. Store oysters for up to 2 days. The closer you buy them to eating time the better. Store in the refrigerator covered with a clean damp tea towel or cloth and then covered with plastic wrap.

simple christmas

Being short on time doesn't mean you have to compromise on flavour or style. This fuss-free menu will ensure your easiest Christmas ever is also one of your best.

NIBBLES

flavoured olives ✱ chicken skewers with preserved lemon

STARTER

✱ roasted prosciutto and bocconcini salad

MAIN

✱ roast pork rack with apples and sage

SIDES

green bean, rocket and parmesan salad
mustard cream ✱ muffin stuffing ✱ coleslaw

DESSERTS

poached fruits in vanilla syrup ✱ amaretti biscuits

combined menu serves 8

chicken skewers with preserved lemon   flavoured olives

roasted prosciutto and bocconcini salad

chicken skewers with preserved lemon

3 chicken breasts, trimmed and thinly sliced
2 tablespoons olive oil
½ cup preserved lemons, flesh removed
  and skin finely chopped
1 clove garlic, crushed
1 teaspoon dried chilli flakes
1½ tablespoons finely chopped thyme
1½ tablespoons finely chopped oregano
sea salt and cracked black pepper
24 bamboo skewers, soaked in water

Place the chicken, oil, lemon, garlic, chilli flakes, thyme, oregano, salt and pepper in a non-metallic bowl and mix well to combine. Thread the chicken onto the skewers. Cook on a preheated hot char-grill (broiler) for 1–2 minutes each side or until golden and cooked through. Makes 24.

+ cook's note Whole preserved lemons in brine are available at delicatessens. Only use the skin in cooking as the flesh will be salty and overly bitter because of the brine.

flavoured olives

250g (8¾ oz) kalamata olives
250g (8¾ oz) green olives
1 tablespoon shredded lemon rind
1 tablespoon thyme leaves
1 teaspoon cracked black pepper
¼ cup (2 fl oz) lemon juice
2 large red chillies, chopped
2 tablespoons olive oil

Combine the olives, lemon rind, thyme, pepper, lemon juice, chilli and olive oil. Allow to marinate for at least 4 hours or preferably overnight. Store in an airtight container in the refrigerator for up to 1 week. Serve with pre-dinner drinks. Serves 8.

roasted prosciutto and bocconcini salad

12 bocconcini (see glossary), halved
12 slices prosciutto (see glossary), halved
8 large slices crusty bread
cracked black pepper
olive oil for drizzling
1 bunch rocket (arugula), trimmed
6 roma tomatoes, sliced
⅓ cup basil leaves
2 tablespoons olive oil, extra
2 tablespoons balsamic vinegar

Preheat the oven to 200ºC (390ºF). Wrap each piece of bocconcini in a slice of prosciutto. Place the bread on a baking tray lined with baking (parchment) paper and top with the wrapped bocconcini. Sprinkle with the pepper and drizzle with the olive oil. Bake for 10 minutes or until the prosciutto is golden. Serve with the rocket, tomatoes and basil tossed in the olive oil and vinegar. Serves 8.

roast pork rack with apples and sage

2kg (4½ lb) pork rack (10 cutlets), with skin on
¼ cup (2 fl oz) olive oil
sea salt
4 green apples, cored and quartered
2 tablespoons sage leaves
2 tablespoons lemon juice
2 tablespoons brown sugar

Preheat the oven to 220ºC (425ºF). Use a sharp knife to score the pork skin at small intervals. Rub the pork generously with the oil and salt. Place the pork on a rack in a baking dish and roast for 30 minutes or until the skin starts to crackle. Reduce the temperature to 200ºC (390ºF) and roast for a further 25 minutes. Place the apples, sage, lemon juice and sugar in a bowl and toss to combine. Add the apples to the base of the dish and roast with the pork for a further 25 minutes or until the pork is cooked through and the apples are tender. Serves 8.

roast pork rack with apples and sage

mustard cream

300g (10½ oz) sour cream
⅓ cup seeded mustard
2 teaspoons finely grated lemon rind
sea salt and cracked black pepper

Place the sour cream, mustard, lemon rind, salt and pepper in a bowl and mix to combine. Refrigerate until required. Serves 8.

coleslaw

¾ white cabbage
6 green onions (scallions), thinly sliced
½ cup flat-leaf parsley leaves
12 radishes, thinly sliced
cracked black pepper
dressing
2 eggs
1½ tablespoons white wine vinegar
3 teaspoons salted capers (see glossary), rinsed
½ cup (4 fl oz) vegetable oil

To make the dressing, process the eggs, vinegar and capers in a food processor until smooth. With the motor running, gradually pour in the vegetable oil until the dressing is creamy. Set aside.

Slice the cabbage into thin wedges and place on serving plates. Spoon over the dressing and top with the onions, parsley, radishes and cracked black pepper. Serves 8.

green bean, rocket and parmesan salad

1 baguette
olive oil
500g (1 lb) green beans, trimmed and blanched
2 bunches rocket (arugula), trimmed
80g (2¾ oz) butter
¼ cup (2 fl oz) lemon juice
2 teaspoons finely grated lemon rind
sea salt and cracked black pepper
parmesan cheese, to serve

Thinly slice the baguette and brush with the olive oil. Toast under a preheated hot grill (broiler) until golden. Layer the baguette on a serving platter with the beans and rocket. Place the butter, lemon juice, lemon rind, salt and pepper in a small saucepan over low heat and stir until the butter is melted. Spoon over the bean salad and sprinkle with the parmesan to serve. Serves 8.

muffin stuffing

100g (3½ oz) butter
1 brown onion, sliced
2 cloves garlic, crushed
2 tablespoons finely grated lemon rind
⅓ cup chopped chives
½ cup chopped flat-leaf parsley leaves
1 tablespoon chopped sage leaves
1 loaf white bread, crusts removed and roughly torn
2 eggs, lightly beaten

Preheat the oven to 200ºC (390ºF). Heat a large non-stick frying pan over high heat. Add the butter, onion, garlic and lemon rind and cook for 3–4 minutes or until the onions are tender. Add the chives, parsley, sage and bread. Cook for 1 minute. Remove from the heat and stir in the eggs. Spoon the mixture into 12 x ½ cup (4 fl oz) capacity greased muffin tins and bake for 15 minutes or until golden. Makes 12.

mustard cream

green bean, rocket and parmesan salad

coleslaw

muffin stuffing

49

poached fruits in vanilla syrup

6 peaches
6 nectarines
6 apricots
2 ²/₃ cups raspberries
2 ²/₃ cups blueberries
vanilla syrup
3 cups (24 fl oz) water
1½ cups granulated sugar
2 vanilla beans (see glossary), split and scraped

To blanch the stone fruit, place the peaches, nectarines
and apricots in batches in a saucepan of boiling water for
30–60 seconds. Carefully remove the skins and set aside.
  To make the vanilla syrup, place the water, sugar and
vanilla beans in a saucepan over medium heat and stir until
the sugar is dissolved. Simmer until the liquid is reduced by
half. Pour the hot syrup over the blanched fruit and allow to
cool. To serve, toss the raspberries and blueberries through
the stone fruit and place in bowls. Remove the vanilla
beans and spoon the syrup over the fruit. Serves 8.

amaretti biscuits

200g (7 oz) raw almonds
1 cup caster (superfine) sugar
¼ cup plain (all-purpose) flour
2 eggwhites
1 teaspoon vanilla extract

Preheat the oven to 180°C (355°F). Process the almonds
and sugar in a food processor until the almonds are roughly
chopped. Add the flour, eggwhites and vanilla and process
until combined. Roll tablespoonfuls of the mixture into balls,
place on a baking tray lined with non-stick baking (parchment)
paper and flatten slightly. Bake for 13 minutes or until lightly
golden. Cool on trays and store in an airtight container for
up to a week. Serve with coffee. Makes 24.

poached fruits in vanilla syrup

amaretti biscuits

simple menu: planning ahead

1 week before

- ☐ Order the pork from your butcher. When storing the pork in your refrigerator, keep it skin-side up so the skin stays dry, thereby ensuring a really crispy crackling.

- ☐ Make the amaretti biscuits and store in an airtight container.

- ☐ Marinate the olives and store in the refrigerator. Allow to stand at room temperature for 20 minutes before serving with drinks.

- ☐ Decide on and purchase the wines, aperitifs, beers and soft drinks to serve with your menu.

3 days before

- ☐ Make the mustard cream and store, covered, in the refrigerator.

- ☐ Shop for all fresh fruit and vegetables.

1 day before

- ☐ Thread the chicken onto the skewers, pour over the marinade and refrigerate.

- ☐ Prepare the poached fruits and refrigerate in the vanilla syrup. (Add the berries just before serving.)

- ☐ Make the muffin stuffing and store in an airtight container in the refrigerator. Reheat uncovered in a 180°C (355°F) oven for 5 minutes before serving.

- ☐ Blanch the beans for the green bean, rocket and parmesan salad and refrigerate.

- ☐ Toast the baguette for the green bean salad and, once cooled, store in an airtight container.

- ☐ Make the dressing for the green bean salad and refrigerate.

- ☐ Make the dressing for the coleslaw and refrigerate.

on the day

- ☐ Wrap the prosciutto and bocconcini parcels and place on a baking tray. Refrigerate until required and bake just before serving. Prepare the rocket, basil and tomato salad and refrigerate.

- ☐ Cook the chicken skewers, allow to cool and refrigerate. Cover with foil and reheat in a hot oven for 3 minutes.

- ☐ Make the coleslaw, pour over the dressing and refrigerate until required.

- ☐ Prepare the pork and place in the oven 1½ hours before serving.

+ perfect pork

The secret to a crackling crisp pork skin over tender, juicy meat is to begin the cooking process at a very high heat (200–220°C/ 390–425°F). Cook for 30 minutes or until the pork skin has bubbled and is crisp. Then reduce the temperature to 180°C (355°F) to cook the meat. Take care not to overcook or it will become dry and tough. There should still be some pink juices running through the meat.

sweet treats

Whether you're hosting a day of celebration, visiting
friends and family or waiting for guests to drop by over the
holidays, a choice of festive little goodies will make their
day. The best thing about this selection is that you can
make them in advance so you'll be ready to join in the fun.
Serve your sweet treats with afternoon tea, hot chocolate
or eggnog … or wrap as a gift with the personal touch.

BISCUITS

✳.

SLICES

✳.

TARTS

✳.

SWEETS

✳.

PUDDINGS

fruit almond tarts   individual christmas puddings

fruit mince pies

fruit almond tarts

90g (3 oz) butter, softened
¼ cup caster (superfine) sugar
1 egg
1 egg yolk, extra
1¼ cups almond meal (see glossary)
1½ tablespoons plain (all-purpose) flour
½ cup raspberries or blueberries
1 tablespoon icing (confectioner's) sugar

Preheat the oven to 150°C (300°F). Place the butter and sugar in the bowl of an electric mixer and beat until pale and creamy. Add the egg, egg yolk, almond meal and flour and beat until smooth. Grease 4 x 10cm (4 in) round tart tins and spoon in the mixture. Smooth the tops and sprinkle over the raspberries or blueberries. Gently press the berries into the filling, sprinkle with icing sugar and bake for 35–40 minutes or until golden. Store in an airtight container for up to 3 days. Makes 4.

individual christmas puddings

1 quantity christmas pudding mixture (see page 24)
8 x 30cm (12 in) squares calico cloth (see glossary)
8 tablespoons plain (all-purpose) flour

Prepare the pudding mixture. Wearing rubber gloves, dip a square of fabric into boiling water and carefully squeeze to remove excess moisture. While the cloth is hot, rub a tablespoon of flour into the centre to form a skin around the pudding. Place 250g (8¾ oz) of pudding mixture in the centre of the cloth and tie with kitchen string to secure. Repeat for the remaining puddings. Boil the puddings in a large saucepan of boiling water for 1 hour 30 minutes, remove from the pan and hang in a cool, dry place until dry. To serve, reheat the puddings in a saucepan of boiling water for 30 minutes. Unwrap and serve with brandy and vanilla custard (see page 24) or brandy butter (see page 64). Keep the puddings in their cloths in plastic wrap in the refrigerator for up to 1 month. Makes 8.

fruit mince pies

700g (1½ lb) ready-prepared shortcrust pastry (see glossary)
1 egg, lightly beaten
caster (superfine) sugar for sprinkling
fruit filling
1 large apple, peeled, cored and grated
⅓ cup sultanas
¼ cup candied peel
⅓ cup currants
⅓ cup slivered almonds
½ cup brown sugar
1 teaspoon mixed spice
30g (1 oz) butter, melted
2 tablespoons sherry

To prepare the fruit filling, place the apple, sultanas, candied peel, currants, almonds, sugar, mixed spice, butter and sherry in a bowl. Mix well, cover and refrigerate for 24 hours.

Preheat the oven to 180°C (355°F). Roll out the pastry until 2mm (⅛ in) thick. Cut into 7cm (2¾ in) rounds using a cookie cutter and place in shallow patty tins. Place 3 teaspoons of fruit mixture in each tart. Cut stars from the remaining pastry and place on top of the fruit mixture. Brush with the egg, sprinkle with the sugar and bake for 15 minutes or until golden. Store in an airtight container for up to 10 days. Makes 22.

simple shortbread

180g (6 oz) cold butter, chopped
¾ cup caster (superfine) sugar
1 cup cornflour (cornstarch), sifted
1½ cups plain (all-purpose) flour, sifted
1 egg

Preheat the oven to 160°C (320°F). Place the butter, sugar, cornflour, flour and egg in a food processor and process until smooth. Press the mixture into a shallow 20 x 30cm (8 x 12 in) tin lined with baking (parchment) paper. Score the top into bars. Bake for 35–40 minutes or until golden. Cool in the tin. Store in an airtight container for 1 week. Makes 16.

simple shortbread

chocolate truffles

½ cup (4 fl oz) (single or pouring) cream
300g (10½ oz) dark couverture chocolate, chopped
cocoa powder, for dusting

Place the cream in a saucepan over medium heat and bring almost to the boil. Add the chocolate and stir for 1 minute. Remove from the heat and stir until smooth. Pour into a greased 15cm (6 in) square cake tin lined with non-stick baking (parchment) paper and refrigerate for 2 hours or until firm. To serve, cut into squares and dust with the cocoa powder. Store in the refrigerator for 10 days. Stand at room temperature for 20 minutes before serving. Makes 16.

pistachio and cranberry nougat

2½ cups caster (superfine) sugar
1 cup (8 fl oz) liquid glucose (available from supermarkets
   and health food stores)
⅓ cup (2½ fl oz) honey
confectionery rice paper (see glossary)
2 eggwhites
200g (7 oz) pistachio nuts, shelled
110g (4 oz) dried sweetened cranberries (see glossary)

Place the sugar, glucose and honey in a saucepan over medium heat and stir until the sugar begins to dissolve. Increase the heat and boil the mixture for 7 minutes or until 140°C (285°F) on a sugar (candy) thermometer.

Line the base of a 20cm (8 in) square cake tin with rice paper. Place the eggwhites in the bowl of an electric mixer and whisk until stiff peaks form. Add the sugar mixture in a thin, steady stream, beating constantly until the mixture is very thick. Fold in the pistachios and dried cranberries and spoon into the tin. Cover the nougat with rice paper and press to flatten. Set aside in a dry place for 8 hours or until set (do not refrigerate). To serve, remove the nougat from the tin and cut into squares. Store in a paper-lined airtight container away from moisture. Again, do not refrigerate. Makes 36 squares.

christmas muffins

2 cups plain (all-purpose) flour
2 teaspoons baking powder
1 teaspoon ground cinnamon
½ cup caster (superfine) sugar
300g (10½ oz) sour cream
1 egg
3 tablespoons vegetable oil
¾ cup dried sweetened cranberries (see glossary)
1 cup halved pitted cherries (fresh or from a jar)

Preheat the oven to 200°C (390°F). Place the flour, baking powder, cinnamon and sugar in a bowl and mix well. Place the sour cream, egg and oil in a bowl and whisk well. Add to the flour mixture with the cranberries and cherries and mix until just combined. Wrap 6 x 1 cup (8 fl oz) capacity ramekins with non-stick baking (parchment) paper, to make tall cylinders (see photo) and secure with string. Spoon the mixture into the ramekins and bake for 30 minutes or until cooked when tested with a skewer. Makes 6.

vanilla snap biscuits

185g (6½ oz) butter
1 cup caster (superfine) sugar
1½ teaspoons vanilla extract
2½ cups plain (all-purpose) flour
1 egg
1 egg yolk, extra
icing (confectioner's) sugar to serve

Preheat the oven to 180°C (355°F). Process the butter, sugar and vanilla in a food processor until smooth. Add the flour, egg and yolk and process to form a dough. Knead lightly, wrap in plastic wrap and refrigerate for 30 minutes. Roll the dough between 2 sheets of non-stick baking (parchment) paper until 5mm (¼ in) thick. Use cookie cutters to cut into shapes. Place on baking trays lined with non-stick baking (parchment) paper. Bake for 10–12 minutes. Cool on wire racks and dust with icing sugar. Store in an airtight container for 1 week. Makes 45.

chocolate truffles

christmas muffins

pistachio and cranberry nougat

vanilla snap biscuits

61

berry and brioche bake

brandy butter

panforte

berry and brioche bake

30g (1 oz) butter
1 tablespoon granulated sugar
1 brioche loaf (see glossary), cut into thick slices
500g (1 lb) strawberries, trimmed and halved
150g (5¼ oz) blueberries
⅓ cup (2½ fl oz) muscat
3 tablespoons caster (superfine) sugar

Preheat the oven to 180°C (355°F). Brush a 23 x 18cm
(9 x 7 in) baking dish with the butter and sprinkle the
granulated sugar over the base. Line the base with the
brioche slices. Combine the strawberries, blueberries, muscat
and caster sugar in a bowl. Spoon over the brioche and bake
for 35 minutes or until the berries are soft and the brioche is
golden. Serve warm or cold with thick cream or vanilla bean
ice cream. Serves 8.
+ cook's note You can also use slices of panettone instead
   of the brioche.

brandy butter

250g (8¾ oz) butter, softened
⅔ cup icing (confectioner's) sugar, sifted
2 tablespoons brandy
1 teaspoon vanilla extract

Beat the butter, icing sugar, brandy and vanilla extract in the
bowl of an electric mixer for 7–10 minutes or until light and
creamy. Store covered in the refrigerator for up to 1 week.
Serves 8.

panforte

1 cup blanched almonds
¾ cup hazelnuts
1 cup chopped dried apricots
1½ cups plain (all-purpose) flour, sifted
¼ cup cocoa powder, sifted
1 teaspoon cinnamon
¼ teaspoon allspice
1 cup (8 fl oz) honey
1 cup caster (superfine) sugar
confectionery rice paper sheets (see glossary), for lining

Preheat the oven to 180°C (355°F). Place the almonds
and hazelnuts on separate baking trays and bake for
5 minutes or until golden. Set the almonds aside. Place
the hazelnuts in a clean tea towel and rub to remove the
skins. Roughly chop the almonds and hazelnuts. Place
the apricots, flour, cocoa, cinnamon and allspice in a
large, heatproof bowl. Set aside.
   Place the honey and sugar in a saucepan and stir over
a low heat until the sugar is dissolved. Brush the sides
of the pan with a pastry brush dipped in water to remove
any sugar crystals. Increase the heat to high and allow
the mixture to simmer for 1–2 minutes or until it reaches
113–115°C (235–240°F) on a sugar (candy) thermometer.
Pour into the flour mixture, add the almonds and hazelnuts
and stir quickly to combine. Line a 20 x 30cm (8 x 12 in)
slice tin with sheets of rice paper and trim the edges to
fit. Press the mixture into the tin. Cook for 20 minutes or
until springy. Cool in the tin. Cut into squares. Store in an
airtight container for up to 2 weeks. Makes 24.

christmas keepsake

Keep a record of your festivities … note down your recipes,

add a few family favourites and make sure this Christmas

is one you'll remember for years to come.

✳.

our christmas _____ year _____

location _____

guest list _____

_____   _____

_____   _____

_____   _____

_____   _____

_____   _____

_____   _____

_____   _____

recipes cooked _____

_____   _____

_____   _____

_____   _____

_____   _____

_____   _____

_____   _____

_____   _____

wines served _____

_____   _____

_____   _____

_____   _____

_____   _____

_____   _____

our christmas

year

location

guest list

recipes cooked

wines served

our christmas _____ year _____

location _____

guest list _____

_____   _____

_____   _____

_____   _____

_____   _____

_____   _____

_____   _____

_____   _____

recipes cooked _____

_____   _____

_____   _____

_____   _____

_____   _____

_____   _____

_____   _____

_____   _____

_____   _____

wines served _____

_____   _____

_____   _____

_____   _____

_____   _____

our christmas _____ year _____

location _____

guest list _____

_____   _____

_____   _____

_____   _____

_____   _____

_____   _____

_____   _____

_____   _____

_____   _____

recipes cooked _____

_____   _____

_____   _____

_____   _____

_____   _____

_____   _____

_____   _____

_____   _____

_____   _____

wines served _____

_____   _____

_____   _____

_____   _____

_____   _____

_____   _____

our christmas _____ year _____

location _____

guest list _____

_____   _____
_____   _____
_____   _____
_____   _____
_____   _____
_____   _____
_____   _____

recipes cooked _____

_____   _____
_____   _____
_____   _____
_____   _____
_____   _____
_____   _____
_____   _____
_____   _____

wines served _____

_____   _____
_____   _____
_____   _____
_____   _____

our christmas _____ year _____

location _____

guest list _____

_____   _____

_____   _____

_____   _____

_____   _____

_____   _____

_____   _____

_____   _____

recipes cooked _____

_____   _____

_____   _____

_____   _____

_____   _____

_____   _____

_____   _____

_____   _____

wines served _____

_____   _____

_____   _____

_____   _____

_____   _____

_____   _____

our christmas _____ year _____

location _____

guest list _____

_____   _____
_____   _____
_____   _____
_____   _____
_____   _____
_____   _____
_____   _____

recipes cooked _____

_____   _____
_____   _____
_____   _____
_____   _____
_____   _____
_____   _____
_____   _____

wines served _____

_____   _____
_____   _____
_____   _____
_____   _____
_____   _____

our christmas   year

location

guest list

recipes cooked

wines served

notes

notes

almond meal

A richer alternative to flour made from ground almonds. Primarily for cakes and desserts but can also be used to thicken sauces or coat meat and fish for frying.

bocconcini

Fresh Italian mozzarella balls, usually made from cows' milk. Sold in a whey liquid at supermarkets and delicatessens.

brioche

A sweet French bread made in a loaf or bun. Traditionally dunked in coffee at breakfast. Available from speciality bread stores and some supermarkets.

calico cloth

An inexpensive, unbleached natural fabric available at home furnishing stores and in haberdashery departments. It is tough enough to withstand the boiling process and won't shrink.

capers

The small, green flower buds of the caper bush. Available packed in brine or salt. Use salt-packed capers when possible, as the texture is firmer and the flavour superior. Rinse thoroughly before use.

cranberries, dried

Sweetened to reduce their tart flavour and perfect for baking and confectionery. Available from the dried fruit section of large supermarkets and health food stores.

kipfler potatoes

Small, long or oval potatoes with yellow skin and flesh that holds its shape when boiled. Toss warm in a dressing for perfect potato salad.

pancetta

A cured and rolled Italian-style meat that is similar to prosciutto but less salty and with a softer texture. It adds a rich flavour when cooked and can be eaten raw in thin slices.

prosciutto

Italian ham that has been salted and air-dried for up to 2 years. The paper-thin slices are eaten raw or used to flavour cooked dishes. Substitute with thinly sliced smoked bacon.

rice paper (confectionery)

A translucent, edible paper made from water and the pith of the rice-paper tree. Flavourless, it can be used to wrap nougat or line patty tins and eaten along with the cakes or confectionery.

rice (stick) noodles

A common ingredient in southeast Asian cooking. Rice noodles are available fresh or dried. Depending on their thickness, rice noodles need only be boiled briefly, or simply soaked in hot water before use.

risotto, basic

Place 6 cups (48 fl oz) chicken stock in a pan over medium heat. Cover and bring to a simmer. Heat a large pan over medium heat, add 20g (¾ oz) butter, 1 tablespoon olive oil and 1 chopped brown onion and cook for 6 minutes or until soft and golden. Add 2 cups arborio rice to the onion mixture, stirring for 2 minutes or until the grains are translucent and coated. Add the hot stock to the rice 1 cup (8 fl oz) at a time, stirring continuously until each cup of stock is absorbed and the rice is al dente (around 25–30 minutes). Stir through ½ cup grated parmesan cheese, 20g (¾ oz) butter, sea salt and cracked black pepper. Serves 4.

scoring

A method of preparation that involves running the point of a knife over the surface of meat or seafood in a cross-hatch formation so that it cuts about halfway through. Commonly used when preparing leg ham for glazing.

shortcrust pastry

Process 2 cups plain (all-purpose) flour with 145g (5 oz) butter in a food processor until the mixture resembles fine breadcrumbs. With the motor running, add enough iced water to form a dough. Knead lightly then wrap in plastic wrap and refrigerate for 30 minutes. Roll to 2mm (⅛ in) thick. Makes 350g (12 oz).

vanilla bean

The pod of an orchid vine native to Central America. It is added, either whole or split, to hot milk or cream to allow the flavour to infuse. Available from specialty food stores, supermarkets and delicatessens.

conversion chart

1 teaspoon = 5ml
1 Australian tablespoon = 20ml
  (4 teaspoons)
1 UK tablespoon = 15ml
  (3 teaspoons/½ fl oz)
1 cup = 250ml (8 fl oz)

liquid conversions

metric	imperial	cups
30ml	1 fl oz	⅛ cup
60ml	2 fl oz	¼ cup
80ml	2¾ fl oz	⅓ cup
125ml	4 fl oz	½ cup
185ml	6 fl oz	¾ cup
250ml	8 fl oz	1 cup
375ml	12 fl oz	1½ cups
500ml	16 fl oz	2 cups
600ml	20 fl oz	2½ cups
750ml	24 fl oz	3 cups
1 litre	32 fl oz	4 cups

cup measures

1 cup almond meal	110g	3½ oz
1 cup breadcrumbs, fresh	50g	2 oz
1 cup sugar, brown	200g	6½ oz
1 cup sugar, white	225g	7 oz
1 cup caster (superfine) sugar	225g	7 oz
1 cup icing (confectioner's) sugar	125g	4 oz
1 cup plain (all-purpose) flour	125g	4 oz
1 cup rice flour	100g	3½ oz
1 cup rice, cooked	165g	5½ oz
1 cup arborio rice, uncooked	220g	7 oz
1 cup basmati rice, uncooked	220g	7 oz
1 cup couscous, uncooked	180g	6 oz
1 cup lentils, red, uncooked	200g	6½ oz
1 cup polenta, fine, uncooked	180g	6 oz
1 cup basil leaves	45g	1½ oz
1 cup coriander (cilantro) leaves	40g	1¼ oz
1 cup mint leaves	35g	1¼ oz
1 cup flat-leaf parsley leaves	40g	1¼ oz
1 cup cashews, whole	150g	5 oz
1 cup cooked chicken, shredded	150g	5 oz
1 cup olives	175g	6 oz
1 cup parmesan cheese, finely grated	100g	3½ oz
1 cup green peas, frozen	170g	5½ oz

donna hay is an Australian-based food stylist, author and magazine editor and one of the best-known names in cookbook and magazine publishing in the world. Her previous eight books have sold more than 2.2 million copies internationally and are renowned for their fresh style, easy-to-follow recipes and inspirational photography. These best-selling, award-winning titles – including *the instant cook, modern classics book 1, modern classics book 2* and *off the shelf* – together with *donna hay magazine* have captured the imagination of cooks worldwide and set a new benchmark in modern food styling and publishing.